The 10 Must-Know Stories

Written by
Heather Butler

Illustrated by
David Mostyn

© Heather Butler 2008
First published 2008, reprinted 2009, 2015

ISBN 978 1 84427 326 3

All rights reserved. No part of this publication may be reproduced, stored in a retrieval system, or transmitted in any form or by any means, electronic, mechanical, photocopying, recording or otherwise, without the prior permission of Scripture Union.

The right of Heather Butler to be identified as author of this work has been asserted by her in accordance with the Copyright, Designs and Patents Act 1988.

British Library Cataloguing-in-Publication Data.
A catalogue record of this book is available from the British Library.

Printed in India by Thomson Press India Ltd

Cover design by Paul Airy
Internal design and layout by Helen Jones
Cover and internal illustrations by David Mostyn

Scripture Union is an international Christian charity working with churches in more than 130 countries.

Thank you for purchasing this book. Any profits from this book support SU in England and Wales to bring the good news of Jesus Christ to children, young people and families and to enable them to meet God through the Bible and prayer.

Find out more about our work and how you can get involved at:
www.scriptureunion.org.uk (England and Wales)
www.suscotland.org.uk (Scotland)
www.suni.co.uk (Northern Ireland)
www.scriptureunion.org (USA)
www.su.org.au (Australia)

The beginning of time

In the very beginning, long before what we know ever existed, God brought his world into being. It hung, surrounded by darkness, without form or shape, suspended in space.

> Let there be light!

These were the very first words spoken into the universe at the start of time. These words were powerful enough to separate darkness and light. The light was good. So was the darkness. God knew the world would need both. He was planning ahead.

> Let there be a space with water above it and below.

The second day had dawned. God had spoken again and droplets of water began to rise. Clouds arched their backs, playing for the first time in the newly formed sky. Rain splashed in the rolling waves below.

> Let the water below the sky come together in one place to create land.

Explosions erupted as mountains, canyons, ice caps, volcanoes and deserts were carved into existence. Plants, fruit trees, grain, grass and bushes sprang up. All these were in place as the third day came to its close.

Planet Earth joined other planets spinning round the dazzling sun. Golden beams gave warmth and light. The silvery softness of the moon and stars took over at night. Evening and morning – the fourth day.

> Let the waters be full to overflowing with living creatures. Let the air be filled with birds.

Energy and life swooped and swirled and leapt and played until evening came. And even then, it didn't stop – the fifth day.

> I command there to be every kind of tame and wild animal and reptiles too.

And there they were, darting and chasing, brilliant and different.

Trunks slurped up water, voices brayed and twittered and croaked, babies squeaked and squalled.

There were long necks, pointed beaks, black and white stripes, yellow spots and skins that changed colour.

Animals swung from trees, burrowed into the ground and rolled in the mud.

They were everywhere.
When God had finished he looked at what he had done and smiled.
He was very pleased and ready for the final piece of creation.

> Now we will make people.

God made men and he made women. When he spoke his voice was full of pleasure, for he loved the people he had made and gave them his blessing.

"You are to be the gardener," he said. "Take care of everything and enjoy it. Have lots of children and enjoy them. There are lots of different kinds of food to eat. Enjoy that too!"

God gave every single thing to the people he had created. Yes, from molehills to mountains, ice caps to waterfalls, daytime to night-time, slimy toads to leathery rhinos, and garden sparrows to golden eagles. By the seventh day God had finished his work so he rested. That made it a special day.

And then... the serpent arrived, a beanpole of a creature with a flickering tail. He had come to Eden, in the East, to see what was going on in this garden. He was not pleased with what he found. He didn't think it was beautiful and fun! He hated watching people laughing and enjoying themselves and as for talking with God, that was the worst thing of all.

Right in the middle of the garden the serpent saw a tree. God had told the people to eat fruit from any other tree, but not this one. With a bit of craft and cunning, the serpent thought, he might persuade them to do the opposite of what God had said. So he wrapped himself around the tree. He wanted to talk with the woman, eyeball to eyeball.

"Did God really tell you not to eat fruit from any tree in the garden?" he hissed softly.

"God said we could eat from any tree in the garden except the one in the middle." The woman's voice was soft yet firm.

"And...?" The serpent's question hung in the air.

"He told us if we ate fruit from this tree, we would die." The serpent's tongue flicked. His head drew a large circle in the air.

"Hey, you won't die! Just look at the fruit on this tree. It is delicious. Come on! Take just one bite. You will begin to understand some new things. You'll be more like God. You'll know the difference between good and bad."

The woman shook her head as the serpent swayed gently.

"Go on," he murmured, "just one bite."

The woman hesitated then slowly raised her arm and picked a fruit from the branch nearest her. She held it in her hand, studied it, sank her teeth into it, chewed… then swallowed. Silently the serpent slipped back down the tree. The woman immediately called the man over. He must try this fruit too. He took a big bite, he chewed… and swallowed.

The man looked at the woman. The woman looked at the man. They both felt bad, really awful inside, like they had never felt before. They wanted to find clothes to cover themselves up. It was cold and they were embarrassed.

"Where are you?" God's voice called out, later that day. The man scuttled out from behind a tree. They had never hidden from God before.

"Have you eaten any of the fruit from the tree in the middle of the garden?"

"It was the woman's fault, so don't blame me. She called me over. She gave it to me! She'd already tried it."

"The serpent tricked me," the woman whispered, hiding behind the man.

The serpent was unable to hide. "You know what you have done, don't you?" God said to the serpent. "You will crawl on your stomach for ever and will eat dust. You and the woman will hate each other." The sadness in God's voice was almost deafening.

The serpent dropped to the ground like fruit falling from a tree. He slithered away.

God still loved the people he had made. He led them out of the garden and made clothes for them, much better than the ones they had made for themselves. But life was going to be tough from now on. Nothing would ever be the same.

Boat building on dry land

Fighting, stealing, cheating, bullying – in every corner of the earth, it seemed like everything people thought and did was bad. In the end God said, "I'm sorry I ever made them." Then he looked around to see if there was anyone left who might take him seriously.

And he saw… Noah. An ordinary man who believed in God enough to listen and then do what he was told. He was also strong enough to cope with being laughed at. Noah was God's man.
"I'm going to destroy everyone," God told Noah.
Imagine Noah's face when he heard that. Then imagine his face when he heard the next bit.
"Get some strong wood and build a boat. You're going to build it on dry land, not water. Put rooms in it and give it a roof to keep out the rain. Make it 133 m long, (longer than a football pitch), 22 m wide, (twice the distance from the penalty spot to the goal line) and 13 m high, (higher than a pile of three double-decker buses). Make it three floors high with just one door on the side. I promise that all your family – you, your wife, your three sons and their wives – will be kept safe in the boat."
God went on. "When you go into the boat take with you a male and female of every kind of animal, bird and reptile that there is. And food to feed them all."
Noah liked animals. That was another reason God had chosen him. He was going to be a master builder, a ship's captain and a chief zookeeper. He was going to be very busy.
Noah needed so much wood that he had to ship in logs from forests far away. (Well not 'ship' exactly since this was all on dry land.) He mixed bucketloads of tar to daub on the outside walls, the roof and then the insides as well.

While he was doing this, people came on day trips to see what was happening. They fell about laughing. What madman would build a boat in the middle of dry land? And why build it so long and wide and tall? Then they went home again.

At last the boat was finished. It towered above the trees and fields around it. The day trippers clapped and cheered. "But how will you get it to water?" they called out. "It's too heavy to drag anywhere and too wide for our river."

Noah knew the answer to their question. God had told him that in seven days' time it would begin to rain. It wouldn't stop for 40 days and 40 nights. The earth would be flooded. That meant Noah had just seven days to collect all the animals. That's not very long.

But a week later, Noah, his wife, his three sons and their wives stood by their huge boat now stuffed with noisy, smelly, restless creatures. Was it really going to rain? They still didn't know as they climbed inside. The door banged shut behind them. It was God who had shut the door.

That day the sky opened its windows and the rivers and underground streams burst. The day trippers rushed home, afraid their homes would be washed away. On and on the water gushed until the boat started to float. Before long all the trees and the tracks, the hills and homes disappeared – everything except one tar-covered boat bobbing on the surface of the water.

The pitter-patter on the roof went on and on and on. The water covering the land was unimaginably deep. Did any of the animals inside the boat have babies? Did they get seasick? Did Noah and his wife argue? We'll never know, but we do know that God did not forget them. After 40 days the rain stopped. The silence outside seemed strange after the noisy pitter-patter. Slowly, very slowly, the water levels began to drop. But it took 150 days before Noah heard a scraping sound. The bottom of the boat had struck the rocks on top of the Ararat Mountains.

But Noah waited 40 more days. Then he carried a raven to

the top floor. The raven got very excited when it saw open skies through the gap between the wall and the roof. It unfurled its wings, thought of doing a loop-the-loop, changed its mind and circled high. No way was it going back inside! It kept flying round and round and round for days and days searching for land.

A while later, Noah carried a dove to the top floor. It cooed gently as it squeezed through the gap. Doing wing stretches and press-ups in cramped conditions was no joke. It flew off but before long it came back. It couldn't find any branches to land. So Noah waited another seven days before he released the dove again. This time it flew back with a single green olive leaf in its beak. Noah grinned. Leaves meant trees. Trees meant plants. Plants meant food. Food meant getting off this boat!

Yet still Noah waited one more week. He sent out the dove and this time it didn't return. Noah jumped up and down in excitement. Then he smashed a hole in the roof of the boat and popped his head up. He breathed in huge gulps of fresh air, gasping at the sunlight, the land and the mountains. He was alive. His family was safe.

God told Noah to leave the boat. He couldn't get out fast enough. He felt wobbly to be walking on dry land and stretching his arms wide without hitting anything. The very first thing Noah did was to thank God.

And God said, "I will never again punish the earth like this. As long as the earth remains, people will plant seeds and harvest them. Winter and summer, day and night will come and go. Whenever you see a rainbow, just remember this promise."

Noah looked up. High above him a glorious rainbow arched its back and reached down to the earth – red, orange, yellow, green, blue, indigo, violet. Wow!

The big clean-up

"We'll set up camp right here!"

It was the voice of Moses, the old man who had led the people in their dramatic escape from Egypt. That was two months ago. Since then they had been moving slowly, setting up a camp, moving on again, setting up camp, moving on, setting up camp.

These people were all from one large family, thousands and thousands of them who all shared the same great-, great-, great-, great- (and a few more) grandfather. His name was Israel. They had been slaves in Egypt for almost more years than anyone could remember. Their slave masters had beaten them. Now, it was fantastic to have escaped, but it was scary too. Would life be better? Where were they going? Did Moses really know what he was doing? After all, he was an old man and had grown up as an Egyptian prince. He had never really lived with these people or known what it was like to be a slave. But he had said, "We'll set up camp right here!" So that was what they were doing.

They dropped their bundles and sighed with tiredness. The ground was rough and hard, as you would expect at the bottom of a mountain. But there was a stream close by and there was shelter from the wind. Before long, tents were being put up and places found for the animals to graze. Fires were lit, water was boiling and food was being prepared. This was their life in the desert. But it was better than in Egypt.

Within days of arriving, Moses climbed up the mountain behind the campsite. He met God there. It was all very mysterious but Moses looked fairly cheerful when he reappeared.

"God has told me he will keep us safe if we do what he says. We'll be known as the people of God!" He also said he was going to speak with God and everyone would hear the conversation.

Wow! Actually speak with God! Moses gave some very

clear instructions. They had three days to get themselves ready. Everyone, absolutely everyone, had to wash themselves all over and put on clean clothes. They had to be clean because they were meeting with God who was pure.

Getting ready to meet God was hard work. Their clothes were made out of such heavy cloth that it took ages for them to dry, even in the hot sun.

But three days later everyone, absolutely everyone, had clean bodies and clean clothes. They waited, in the campsite. Children hopped from one foot to another. Adults whispered anxiously. In the middle of the crowd, a child suddenly pointed at the mountain. Those around followed her finger. Everyone could see. There was no missing it now. The top of the mountain was being covered in a thick, swirling cloud of smoke. No one had ever seen anything like this before. Moses beckoned and led the people towards the foot of the mountain. God's orders were that no one was to step onto the mountain itself.

As they stood there with Moses in front, the loudest, most terrifying blast erupted from inside the mountain. Later they described it as sounding like a trumpet vibrating and exploding in each person's ear. Smoke belched upwards and sideways and out in all directions. Then the earth began to shake and rattle; louder and louder still. The smoke was now hovering just above people's heads, hot and fiery. In the middle of this they heard a voice calling Moses to come back up the mountain.

For an old man, Moses was very strong. The people watched him get smaller and smaller until he disappeared into the smoke. Would he ever come back?

Hours passed and the people waited. Lunchtime came and went. No one ate anything. The afternoon sun began to sink in the sky. And still they waited. At last, they saw a figure moving down the mountain, out of the smoke. It was Moses. In silence they watched him stride towards them.

Somehow, at the top of the mountain, surrounded by the smoke and rumbles, God had spoken to Moses and given him instructions for his people. These instructions were how God, who was pure, wanted his people to behave. So in front of the people, still in their clean clothes (with smoke smuts all over them) Moses told the people what God had said.

One. I am the Lord your God. I brought you out of Egypt where you were slaves. Don't worship any other god except me.
("In other words," someone explained to his children, "remember who God is, so don't be tempted to put your trust in anything or anyone else – not that you're likely to after today.")
Two. Do not make idols.
("In other words," someone else whispered, "don't draw pictures or make statues of God and worship them.")
Three. Do not misuse my name.
("That includes breaking promises after swearing something is true or using God's name when you haven't thought about it. God's name is special.")

Four. Remember I made the world in six days then rested. You must rest every seventh day.
("The rule is six days on, one day off.")
Five. Respect your father and your mother.
("Listen to that one, son. Don't forget it. Families are very important.")
Six. Do not murder.
("Life is a gift from God.")
Seven. Be faithful in marriage.
("Families again.")
Eight. Do not steal.
("Don't take anything that isn't yours.")
Nine. Do not tell lies.
("Be completely honest.")
Ten. Do not look at anything that belongs to someone else and want it for yourself.
("Jealousy is bad for you.")

This was serious stuff. The people had made themselves clean for this day. God now wanted them to go on living clean lives. So the people of God (for that was what they were) walked back to the campsite. No photographs, no videos, no films, no soundtracks, but the memory of this day would be fixed in their minds for ever.

The secret weapon

Question: What sort of things did a shepherd do three thousand years ago?
Answer: He made sure there was grass to munch and water to drink for all his sheep. He protected them from wild animals with his secret weapon, and made sure they didn't get lost. It was an important job but no one, except the sheep themselves, thought shepherds were special.

Question: What was the secret weapon?
Answer: Imagine a strip of leather with a string at each end, like a catapult. The shepherd laid a small stone or pebble on the leather and pulled up the strings. He lifted it up and began spinning, faster and faster and faster. As he released one of the strings, the stone or pebble zipped through the air. Splat! Straight into a fierce, wild animal. This was a shepherd's secret weapon.

Jesse was a farmer and had lots of sons. In fact, he had eight of them. The three oldest were soldiers and they thought they were very important. The youngest was a shepherd and no one except his sheep thought he was important. His name was David. Day after day, he practised killing wild animals using his secret weapon.

David's older brothers, who went by the names of Eliab, Abinadab and Shammah, took themselves off to fight for the Israelite army led by King Saul. The Israelite army was on one side of the Elah Valley. Their enemies, the Philistines, were sprawled out on the other side. Every morning the enemy, in the shape of a whopping sized giant called Goliath, appeared on the opposite hillside and bellowed at the Israelites. Wearing his metal armour, he would swish and swagger through the long grass until he was halfway down the hill.

Then his voice would thunder round the valley. "Oi, you lot, send your best soldier to fight me! If he kills me, my people will be your slaves. But if I kill him, you Israelites will be our slaves."

And every morning Saul's army looked at this metal cage on legs. Every morning not a single one of them moved.

In those days, armies didn't provide much for their soldiers. Families had to send their sons food and weapons and anything else they needed. So Jesse, being a farmer, sent a sack of grain and ten loaves of bread to his three sons. He also sent ten large chunks of cheese to their officer to keep him happy. The delivery boy was David.

One day, just as David was dropping off the food, the metal cage on legs lumbered down the opposite hillside.

"What's that?" David asked. He had never seen anything like it.

"Shhhh!" his brothers whispered as Goliath hollered rude things about God and the Israelites.

"Who is he?" David breathed. But no one answered him. They were too scared. Eventually, one soldier whispered that King Saul had said whoever killed Goliath would marry the king's daughter and never have to pay taxes again.

Wow!

"I'll fight him!" David chirped. "He doesn't scare me!"

David's brothers tried to shut him up. After all, he was only a shepherd boy. But David kept on and on about it and soon King Saul got to hear. He sent for David.

"But you are only a boy!" Saul sighed. "Goliath's been a soldier all his life. And he's a giant!"

"So?" David was unimpressed. "Your majesty, to protect my sheep I chase lions and bears. He's no different and he's making fun of the living God. How dare he? I can kill him. God will keep me safe."

Saul tapped his fingers on his sword. This was the first offer he'd had. At least this scruffy little kid believed in God.

"Go on then," he said, "but you'll wear my armour to keep you safe." David remained unimpressed. The helmet came over his eyes, the sword made his arm ache and the shield was almost as big as he was.

Perhaps the armour of someone shorter would fit. But even the smallest helmet slid down David's nose, the sword was still too heavy and he still couldn't see over the shield. David made up his mind. He was going onto the battlefield, just himself, his secret weapon and the living God. So there!

A stream babbled down the hillside. David bent over, chose five smooth pebbles, checked they were the right size, and then strode towards Goliath.

Goliath didn't notice David at first. He was not expecting someone so small without any armour. When he spotted him he

howled with laughter. "When I've finished with you, I'll feed you to the vultures and wolves and bears!" he roared.

David stood his ground and yelled. "You've come to fight me with a sword and a spear and a dagger. But I've come out to fight you in the name of the living God. I'll knock you down and tear off your head. Everybody will see that God doesn't need swords or spears to save his people."

Question: What do you do if you are small and a giant comes lumbering towards you?
Answer: You load your secret weapon and whizz it round your head. You wait until the giant is close enough so you can see his teeth and hear the leather of his shin pads creaking. Then you release the stone.

Shepherds rarely miss. They practice every day, and as usual, David was deadly accurate. His stone went straight into the middle of the giant's helmet where there was a gap. Goliath needed that gap to be able to see. But from that moment, he didn't see anything ever again.

The Philistine soldiers watched everything. They saw their giant hero lying dead. They ran. The Israelite soldiers watched everything too. They chased after the Philistines. Their feet pounded down the hill. Their lungs gasped as they raced up the other side. They crashed through the tents and weapons and supplies of food the Philistines had left behind. They carried on and won.

After the chase, David came back to the army tents. He was clutching the head of the giant. He was also clutching his secret weapon. He was only a shepherd boy but before long he would be a great king.

Lions' breakfast

Persia, the kingdom of King Darius, was made up of 120 regions. There was a governor in charge of each region. These governors were powerful. What they said happened. To make sure the 120 governors behaved properly, Darius put three even more powerful men in charge of them. One of these was Daniel: Daniel, the young Jewish lad, who had been brought back to Persia after a raid on Israel; Daniel, a foreigner, who had worked so hard he had impressed his masters and been promoted; Daniel, who prayed to God three times a day and who was a good man in a powerful position.

The other governors and officials took a dislike to him. They tried to find something wrong with what he did. But they couldn't. Not a single thing. He was honest and faithful and did everything he was supposed to do. So they came up with a cunning plan.

"We'll never be able to bring any charge against Daniel," they schemed, "unless it is to do with his religion."

A few days later they trotted to King Darius. "Your Majesty, we hope you live for ever." (That was how they greeted kings in those days.) "We think you should make a law forbidding anyone to pray to any god or human being except your good self for the next 30 days. Anyone who prays to someone else should be thrown into a pit full of lions. Order the law, sign it and then it cannot be changed."

King Darius clicked his fingers. The law was written. The law was signed. The law was law and the lions were waiting.

Daniel heard about the new law. His heart thudded against his ribcage but he knew what he must do. That evening after he returned home, he went upstairs as he always did. He prayed in front of the window that faced Jerusalem giving thanks to the God

he believed in.

His enemies watched and smiled. Daniel was trapped.

"He's praying for help," they sneered. "He's going to need it."

"Your Majesty, may you live for ever. Didn't you make a law that forbids anyone to pray to any god or human being except your good self for the next 30 days?"

King Darius leaned back on his chair and cracked the joints on his fingers. Had someone dared ignore one of his laws? "Yes, that is the law I made."

Their moment had come. "That Jew, Daniel, who was brought here as a captive, refuses to obey the law you ordered to be written. He still prays to his god three times a day."

King Darius' brain went ice cold. Daniel was his trusted, faithful friend. Why had he deliberately disobeyed this law?

"Laws cannot be changed, can they, Your Majesty."

The official robes of the enemies swept the floor as they crossed the room. In the shadowy courtyard, where lizards panted in the heat, they whooped for joy. Daniel was dead meat.

Behind them the king stared at the wall. He was trapped. They were right. Laws like this could not be changed. He had no choice but to order Daniel to be taken to the lions' pit. The king himself watched as the guards pushed Daniel, clothes and all, into the pit where sharpened claws and shredding teeth were waiting.

"You've been faithful to your God. I pray that he will rescue you," Darius whispered. He knew he had been tricked, but was Daniel's God powerful enough to save Daniel?

A stone was rolled over the pit and sealed with the king's seal. Darius returned to his palace. Insects chattered as the silver moon slid across the sky. Servants snored in their rooms but sleep did not visit the king that night. He was a troubled man.

At first light, he threw some clothes on and ran to see what had happened. He wrenched the seal off the stone.

"Daniel!" he shouted as the guard shuffled beside him. "Has your God saved you?"

There was no crunching of bones, no munching or chewing of...

"May Your Majesty live forever!" A clear voice echoed from the darkness. "My God has kept me safe. He sent an angel to stop the lions eating me."

DANIEL WAS ALIVE!

"Pull him out of the pit. Let me see him. From now on we will worship this God, who protects people like this."

As Daniel's feet scraped over the side of the pit, the lions began to snarl and roar. They had been stopped from eating their evening meal and now breakfast was disappearing.

"Your God has protected you," King Darius repeated, staring at Daniel who should have been dead. "He's kept you safe!"

Daniel nodded. "That's why I worship only him."

The lions roared!

Surprise, surprise!

Joseph was a carpenter who lived in Nazareth in Galilee, a small village in the north. Soon he was going to marry Mary. Nothing surprising about that because he loved her! But then a whole load of other surprises came his way.

He was surprised (and a bit fed up) to hear that the Roman authorities wanted everyone to go back to where they came from to put their names on a register. He knew why – so they could get people to pay more tax. Joseph packed up his bags to make the 100 km journey to Bethlehem in the south because that was where he came from. Before he went, he made sure his carpenter's workshop would be OK while he was away.

He wasn't going on his own. Mary was going with him. Her baby was due very soon. Now that had been the biggest surprise of all!

All babies are special but Mary's baby was special in a different way. She found out she was going to have the baby when an angel dropped by to see her. A dazzling angel called Gabriel.

"Don't be afraid!" the angel Gabriel said. (Angels spend their lives telling people not to be afraid when they first meet them. That's not surprising when you come to think about it.) "God is pleased with you," Gabriel carried on. "His power will come over you and you will have a son."

"But Joseph and I are not married yet," Mary said when she had got over the shock! (That didn't seem to make any difference.)

"Your child will be called the holy Son of God."

Wow! Mary's heart thudded. The Son of God? Joseph would be surprised.

The angel's neck swayed in a sort of nod.

"OK," Mary whispered. "If that's how God wants it."

So now, quite a few months later, Joseph found himself on the outskirts of Bethlehem, walking beside Mary. Everyone around them was doing the same thing. The town was bustling with laughter as people caught up with friends and family they hadn't seen for ages. Visitors, animals, children and soldiers were everywhere. Mary kept telling Joseph that she thought the baby would be here soon. So Joseph went straight to the home of his relatives. He hoped they would have some space for them to stay. But here came another surprise. They had no room.

So Joseph knocked on a neighbour's door. They had some space in the part of their home where the animals were kept. (In those days, animals and people often lived under the same roof.) Mary could rest on their straw. A few hours later, Mary's baby was born with animals all round. The angel had said the baby would be a boy, and it was. No surprise there!

The baby gulped air into his lungs and cried. Joseph helped Mary wrap him up in strips of cloth which is what new babies

wore in those days. Joseph laid him down in the animals' feeding trough while Mary rested.

In the hills behind the town, some shepherds were doing their everyday (and night) job. Normally it was peaceful with no one but the sheep for company. But tonight was different. Suddenly, and it was sudden, a dazzling angel burst out of nowhere and hovered above them. The shepherds fell flat on the ground and the sheep all pretended to be dead.

The bright light gave the usual greeting. "Don't be afraid!" he said. "A special baby has been born today in Bethlehem. You'll find him lying in a feeding trough."

At this point the noise levels increased as angel voices made the air vibrate with joyful singing. "Peace on earth and praise God in heaven," they sang over and over and over again.

The sheep gasped for breath. The shepherds stood around shocked.

Joseph was in for yet another surprise when he was woken up in the middle of the night by a group of scruffy, out-of-breath shepherds. They stumbled into the room looking for this baby they had been told about. The story they had to tell was amazing.

Eight days later, Joseph took Mary and the baby to the temple where they gave him his name. The angel had told both Mary and Joseph what to call him. It was a name that meant "someone who saves others". No surprise then that the baby was called – Jesus.

And the rest...

Nat and his little brother had chased lizards most of the way up the hill. Their mother kept getting cross with them, telling them to stick to the path. They had come all this way to listen to Jesus, the visiting storyteller, not to chase lizards. Mum had said he was worth listening to. Crowds of other people had had the same idea.

When they reached the grass on the hillside where Jesus was telling his stories, one of Jesus' friends showed them where to sit. They pushed through the crowd and ended up just three rows from the front. It gave them a good view and meant they could hear and see everything. Nat was soon caught up in the stories and cheered with everyone else when Jesus made sick people well again.

As usual, his tummy started rumbling and before long he was asking Mum for something to eat. He knew there were lentils and olives and other bits of food in her basket. Eating these with fingers was messy but mess doesn't matter when you're eating outside.

Nat still felt hungry. "Save the rest for later," his mum said and pulled the basket away.

It was 'the rest' Nat thought about when, much later in the day, he overheard a conversation between two of Jesus' friends, or 'disciples' as Mum called them.

"We'll have to tell Jesus to send the people away so they can go to the villages round here and find food and somewhere to stay."

"This is such a lonely place. Where will they find food?"

Nat frowned. All day Jesus had been making people better. People who couldn't walk were carried up the hill on stretchers. They had run back down the path. Blind people shuffled over towards Jesus helped by friends and family – and then suddenly they could see. Deaf people no longer needed someone to shout at them. Nat didn't quite understand. Surely, making food would be a piece of cake. It would just be like making people better. Why were the disciples saying everyone should go home?

Nat ferreted around in his mother's basket. 'The rest' he was thinking about were some barley loaves and fish. They were a bit squashed. He took them out and tugged at the coat of the disciple standing near to him.

"I've got some small barley bread loaves and some fish here."

"How many?"

"One, two, three, four, five," Nat counted.

"And how many fish?"

"One, two."

The disciple wrinkled his nose, thought a bit, then grinned.

"Come with me," he said.

Nat followed until they stood in front of Jesus. He held out the squashed barley loaves (his brother had sat on them) and the two small fish (they were flat already).

"Here are five loaves and two fish," the disciple spoke into Jesus' ear.

Jesus looked at Nat and then at the bread and fish. They didn't look much at all, but Jesus nodded and smiled.

"Get everyone to sit down in groups of about 50," he said.

Then Jesus held up two of the loaves, one in each hand, looked up to heaven and thanked God for the food. Slowly he began breaking up all five loaves into small pieces. He did the same with the fish. Nat saw what Jesus was doing and gasped. The more Jesus broke up the bread and fish, the more there was. And before long everyone was cheering and holding out their hands as the disciples were giving out the food. Nat was one of the first to get some.

He saved a bit for his brother who had fallen asleep. Mum was going to have to carry him home. That meant Nat would have to carry his mum's basket.

Jesus' friends had begun to pick up the crumbs of food still lying on the ground. In the end they filled twelve huge baskets with the bread and fish pieces. There had been more than enough for everyone to eat. Nat picked up his basket. It was a long walk home!

A good Samaritan

Larry is a lizard. He hangs around waiting for things to happen. Today he is at his favourite place: a big, grey rock next to the road. From there he watches life.

Love this place: flat rock to myself, cool cracks to drop into if it gets too hot, people passing. What else could a lizard ask for? To my left is Jerusalem (23 hours of scurrying). The other way is Jericho (17 hours). People travel from Jerusalem to Jericho and back all the time. I see them all.

And here come the first people of the day. Two men, churning up a cloud of dust behind them, running towards me. Now they've stopped, panting, by my rock. I drop into a crack, then peep out at them. They might be lizard hunters. They're sweating. One has an eyepatch. The other's knuckle is decorated with a deep scar. Something tells me they're bad news.

Eyepatch sees me and turns away. So they are not lizard hunters. But why are they lurking behind my rock? They've stopped whispering. Deep Scar has taken a knife out of his pocket. Eyepatch is clutching a stick. I do not like these two. A man is coming towards us humming a little song. Is he happy or is he nervous?

Eyepatch and Deep Scar have jumped out from behind the rock. They have beaten Humming Man. Now he is lying on the ground in a pool of blood. Why did they kick him so hard? They've stolen his money and are running away. Humming Man is not humming any more. He is dragging himself towards my rock.

Humming Man has pulled his coat over his face. He needs water. It is very hot. The ground is dusty. But, here comes someone who will help, a man walking briskly towards Jerusalem. His fancy clothes are what a priest wears. He must work in the temple. Surely he will be kind. Looks like Humming Man has heard him. He raises his hand. Fancy Dress Man looks across. But he does not stop! He is in a hurry. He walks by very fast, on the other side of the road. I stick my neck out. When I am angry it quivers and goes red. It is red now. Very red. Fancy Dress Man has disappeared down the road. Humming Man's head has flopped back into the dust.

Humming Man's lips are parched. The blood on his face has turned a brownish colour. But here comes someone who might help – one of Fancy Dress Man's friends. He has a different coloured coat but I know he works in the temple too. Humming Man has heard him. He lifts his head a little and moans. But Temple Man ignores him and walks by quickly, on the other side. I stick out my neck again. It has gone even redder than very red.

Humming Man is getting worse. He is not moving any more. I am very worried.

This road has not been very busy today. Here comes what may be Humming Man's last chance – a man on a slowly moving donkey. This man looks like he comes from the region called Samaria. That makes him a Samaritan. Samaritans are hated by people from round here. Humming Man, are you going to be saved by someone you hate? Samaritan has stopped and is sliding off his donkey's back. His knees creak as he kneels beside Humming Man. Samaritan goes back to his donkey. He pulls a piece of cloth out of his bag and rips it up to make a bandage. He's got wine and oil, too.

Samaritan helps Humming Man sit up. He pours oil on his cuts and gives him a drink. Now he is helping him onto the back of his donkey. I had better hang onto the donkey's tail if I am going to see what happens next.

We've stopped at a guest house. It'll be cool inside. Samaritan lifts Humming Man off the donkey. He calls for someone to help carry Humming Man inside. There's a chink of money. Samaritan is paying for Humming Man to stay.

"If you need more money, I will pay you next time I am passing by."

What a hero! Samaritan doesn't even know this man he has helped. He ought to be called "A Good Samaritan"!

The tale of two sons

Jesus sat down. His eyes swept slowly over the crowd who were waiting for another story. Children squeezed to the front, enjoying a family outing. Adults glanced at the temple leaders who were hovering like vultures at the edge of the crowd. They were unhappy with what Jesus said and how he treated everyone in the same way. Why, they asked themselves, did Jesus bother with ordinary people like these? Most of them were no-hopers!

Jesus was ready. The crowd was quiet. The storyteller could begin.

"There was a man with two sons. The younger son was not happy. (The older son was not happy either but more of that later.)

"Give me my share of everything you own," the younger son said to his father one day. Just like that. He knew that when his dad died, everything would be shared between him and his brother. But he wanted the money now. To spend.

To his delight and surprise, his father did as he asked, dividing everything into two equal parts. The older son watched. He saw the smile on his brother's face grow as the pile of money, sheep, goats, bits of furniture, cooking pots, tools and everything else got bigger and bigger and bigger. The older son was not happy. The younger son was.

Smugly, the younger son packed his bags.

"Ta-ra!" he called over his shoulder. Money clinked in his pocket, sheep bleated behind him, cartwheels rattled over the bumpy track. He was taking what was his. He planned to go to a foreign country where no one knew him. There would be no big brother keeping an eye on him and no father watching what he did. His father could be dead for all he cared.

Before long he had a house in his new country. He could do what he liked with his money. And he did – parties, shopping,

more parties, more shopping, a bigger house, a few more parties. His new friends helped him. His new friends were good at helping him – until there was no money left. Then they disappeared. A famine had come to that country, so to add to his troubles there was little food to eat. No money, no food, no friends, no job, no family, no hope – no wonder he was desperate.

At that time, pigs were cared for by no-hopers. There was no worse job. The younger son was so desperate that he went to the local pig farmer and offered to look after the pigs. It got so bad that he even ate the swill of the pigs he was looking after.

One day he said to himself, "My father's workers have plenty to eat back home and here I am, starving to death! I will go to my father and say to him, 'Dad, I have wronged God in heaven and wronged you. I've wasted all your money and treated you dreadfully. I am no longer good enough to be called your son. Can I have a job on the farm because at least your workers have enough to eat?'"

So the younger son set off for home – no money clinking in his pockets, no sheep bleating, no cartwheels rattling over the bumpy track. He was a broken man with just the hope that his father would allow him to work for him.

What the younger son did not know was that at least once a day since he had left home, his father had walked to the edge of the village and stared up the track his son had taken when he left. Every day he hoped his son would come home. And on this particular day he had gone to the edge of the village around lunchtime. He looked up the track and… there was his son, kicking up stones, head bowed, trudging along the road.

The father recognised him immediately. Without a second thought, he charged towards his son. He flung his arms out wide in welcome.

"My son! You've come home!" he yelled, so loud that every one in the village must have heard.

But his son did not run into his father's arms. He did not smile. He didn't even look pleased. Instead he dropped at his father's feet and sobbed.

"I have wronged you and God…" How many times had he practised saying this? "I'm not good enough to be called your son. Can I just be a worker on your farm?"

The father heard the sadness in his voice. It didn't matter to him that his younger son smelt of pigs and sweat, or that he had as good as wished his father dead. He pulled his son to his feet and looked deep into his eyes. Then he hugged him as he had never hugged him before.

The father had forgiven him and to prove it he put a ring on his son's finger. This was a sign of being part of the family. Then he found him some new clothes.

"This son of mine was as good as dead," he kept telling

everyone, "but he's come back to life. It's time for a party!"

Before long, meat sizzled over the fire, the table was spread with the best food, there was music, laughter and dancing. What a party!

But then… the older son came home, as he did every day after working hard in the fields. He hadn't seen his father race along the track. But as he got closer, he smelt meat cooking.

"What's going on?" he asked one of the servants.

"Your brother's come home."

"Why's he come home? And why throw a party for him?"

The servant swallowed hard. This older son was not happy.

Just then his father joined them. "Come on, you're missing the party," he said.

"No way am I going to a party!" the older son spat in rage. "For years I've worked for you. I've done everything you asked me to do. But you've never given a party for my friends. But as soon as this pathetic, selfish brother of mine comes home, that's just what you do! It's not fair!"

The father sighed. "Everything I have is yours. You are always with me. Come on. Your brother's return is worth a celebration!"

Jesus paused. A lizard scurried across the ground. The older brothers at the edge of the crowd muttered to themselves. Why did Jesus tell stories about no-hopers that had happy endings?

He's not a ghost

The best time to arrest someone famous is at night, when no one is expecting it. That's what the religious leaders in Jerusalem thought. They wanted to be rid of Jesus, this man who claimed to be God, who healed sick people, who told stories everyone loved to hear and even had the nerve to tell the religious leaders how God wanted them to behave. What a cheek! He had to go!

So, late one evening when Jesus was outside in a garden praying, and his friends had fallen asleep, soldiers hurriedly arrested him. It was dark and no one was expecting them. The crowds that for weeks had listened to Jesus' every word were fast asleep too. The soldiers dragged Jesus off to prison. His friends tried to defend him but were too afraid to stick by him.

The religious leaders wanted him dead, but first they had to decide on his crime so they could charge him. They ordered Jesus to stand before them. The soldiers had already beaten him up. His face was badly bruised and bleeding.

The religious leaders asked him, "Do you claim to be the Son of God?" (They thought anyone who claimed this was a liar and deserved to die.)

"That's right," Jesus replied.

"He deserves to die," they all shouted. That was a good enough crime for them.

But it was not that simple. It was the Roman authorities who had the power to put criminals to death. So the Romans had to be convinced that Jesus was a troublemaker and deserved to die. (They gladly killed anyone who caused trouble.)

So the religious leaders took Jesus to be judged by the Roman governor. He was called Pontius Pilate.

"What's he done wrong?" Pilate asked. He didn't much like the religious authorities and didn't care if Jesus was God or not.

"He's telling people they don't have to pay taxes to Rome," they said. (That meant trouble.)

"He says he's a king," they added. (That meant serious trouble.)

"He whipped up a crowd to riot," they finished off. (That meant seriously big trouble.)

But Pilate wasn't sure that Jesus deserved to die. He really wanted to let him go. But he was a weak man and Jesus' enemies knew this.

By now it was early in the morning and a crowd had gathered outside. Crowds like to watch famous people in action – which was what Jesus was. The religious leaders were clever though. They whipped up the crowd to scream and shout against Jesus. It looked as though there would be a riot.

There was no way Pilate could let that happen. He went outside where everyone could see him. "Look," he shouted, "I'll give you a choice. At this time of year I have the power to release one prisoner. We can put Barabbas to death. He's a cruel murderer. Or we can put Jesus to death. Who do you want?"

And the mob chanted, "Jesus! Jesus! Put Jesus to death!" So Jesus it was.

Soldiers dragged him out of the city to the place where criminals were nailed by their hands and feet to a wooden cross and left to hang. It was a cruel, slow way to die. That was how Jesus died. He hung there for six hours. Even though it was daytime, there was an eerie darkness as people stood watching, waiting for his death. At three o'clock, he breathed for the last time.

His body hung, lifeless. There was no doubt he was dead. The Roman soldier who was watching made sure of that. Some of Jesus' friends asked permission to take his broken body down from the cross. They placed it in a small cave and a stone was heaved across the entrance. Shocked and stunned they went home. This was not meant to have happened.

Two days later, very early in the morning before it was light, some women who were friends of Jesus, went to the cave. They were carrying sweet-smelling spices to pour over his body. They had no idea how they were going to move the huge stone that blocked the entrance. But when they got there, the stone had already been rolled away. Jesus' body had vanished and angels were sitting there to greet them!

"Why are you looking in a grave for someone who is alive?" the angels asked. "Jesus isn't here! He has been raised from death."

This didn't make sense. Or did it? The women ran from the cave and went to find the disciples.

"He's gone. He's not in the cave," they told them, their words tumbling out in a rush.

"Where is he then?" they asked.

"He's alive. An angel told us!"

"Oh yeah!" the disciples said. They did not believe the women. People as dead as Jesus had been don't come alive again. Surely the women were making it up.

But then that evening, two of Jesus' friends were walking home from Jerusalem. It would take them well over three hours. They were talking about all that had happened. There wasn't much else to talk about. A stranger caught up with them. He didn't seem to know anything about Jesus' death. So they told him all about it. But then this stranger began to explain all the events of the last few days in a fresh way. He made it sound as though everything was going to be OK, that Jesus' death was part of something bigger. They talked so much that before they knew it, they were at the edge of their village. The two men invited the stranger to stay for a meal. As they were eating, he held up bread and broke it. And suddenly the two men realised who the stranger was. At that exact moment, Jesus disappeared.

Well, there was only one thing for these two friends to do. The women had been right! They should have believed them. They raced all the way back to Jerusalem – another three hours – to tell the other disciples.

"We've seen him!" they shouted, bursting into the room. "Jesus is alive!"

"Oh yeah!"

"He is. Believe us." And while they told their story, Jesus himself was right there with them. They all stared at him, open mouthed.

"Touch me," he said. "I'm not a ghost."

Jesus took a mouthful of the baked fish they had been eating and started chewing. They didn't need to touch him. He was no ghost. Jesus was alive.

DEDICATION

Mum, you shared your faith and your gifts with us. Thank you. Without them, this book could not have been written.

These stories are the ten Must Know Stories because people voted them as the ten most important stories to pass on to the next generation – readers like you! You can read them in full in the Bible. Here is where you can find them.

The Old Testament (the first part)
Page 3   The beginning of time – Genesis 1–3
Page 8   Boat building on dry land – Genesis 6–8
Page 12 The big clean-up – Exodus 19–20
Page 17 The secret weapon – 1 Samuel 17
Page 22 Lions' breakfast – Daniel 6

The New Testament (the second part)
Page 26 Surprise, surprise! – Luke 1–2
Page 30 And the rest… – Luke 9:10–17
Page 34 A good Samaritan – Luke 10:25–37
Page 39 The tale of two sons – Luke 15:11–32
Page 44 He's not a ghost – Luke 22–24